The Faces of Americans i

The Faces
of Americans
in 1853

Poems by Wesley McNair

Carnegie Mellon University Press
Pittsburgh 2001

Library of Congress Control Number 00-111583
ISBN 0-88748-356-9
Printed and bound in the United States of America
First Carnegie Mellon University Press Edition,
May 2001

The Faces of Americans in 1853 was first published by
the University of Missouri Press, Columbia, in 1983.

10 9 8 7 6 5 4 3 2 1

For Diane

Acknowledgments

Grateful acknowledgment is made to the following magazines and anthologies in which many of these poems first appeared: *The Atlantic Monthly* for "Mina Bell's Cows" and "Trees That Pass Us in Our Cars"; *The Boston Monthly* for "The Man," "Memory of North Sutton," and "Country People"; *Discover America* for "Rufus Porter by Himself"; *Flowering After Frost* for "Fitz Hugh Lane Goes to the Mast-Head"; *Green House* for "The Last Peaceable Kingdom" and "Rufus Porter, Itinerant Muralist and Inventor, Undertakes a Commission in Bradford Center, N.H."; *Hanging Loose* for "Thinking about Carnevale's Wife"; *Hearse* for "Fire in Enfield"; *Ploughshares* for "Old Trees" and "Calling Harold"; *Poetry* for "Small Towns Are Passing," "The Poetic License," "Hair on Television," and "The Bald Spot"; *Poetry Northwest* for "Going Back to Fifth Grade," "Don Greenwood's Picture in an Insurance Magazine," and "Leaving the Country House to the Landlord." "The Faces of Americans in 1853" and "Memory of Kuhre" are reprinted from *Prairie Schooner* by permission of the University of Nebraska Press. Copyright © 1976 and 1972 by the University of Nebraska Press.

"The Bald Spot" was reprinted in the *1981 Anthology of Magazine Verse & Yearbook of American Poetry* (Monitor Book Company, 1981); "Memory of Kuhre" and "Thinking about Carnevale's Wife" were reprinted in *Flowering After Frost* (Branden Press Inc., 1975).

I want to thank the National Endowment for the Arts for a Creative Writing Fellowship that helped me to complete some of the poems in this book.

I also wish to thank Donald Hall, generous guide and friend.

W. C. M.

All journeys, I think, are the same:
The movement is forward, after a few wavers . . .
And I seem to go backward,
Backward in time . . .

—"Meditations of an Old Woman,"
Theodore Roethke

Contents

Where I Live

Leaving the Country House

Small Towns Are Passing

Small towns are passing
into the rearview
mirrors of our cars.
The white houses
are moving away,
wrapping trees
around themselves,
and stores are taking
their gas pumps
down the street
backwards. Just like that
whole families picnicking
on their lawns tilt
over the hill,
and kids on bikes
ride toward us
off the horizon,
leaving no trace
of where they have gone.
Signs turn back and start
after them. Packs of mailboxes,
like dogs, chase them
around corner after corner.

Old Trees

By the road
in the field
they stand, lifting branches

they cannot remember,
rocking shut
in the wind.

In some other world
they grew such trunks
and hurled their leaves

across the sky.
Now, empty-handed,
they wait

for the end which has been
happening for years.
Nodding off

beside telephone wires,
tethered to farmhouses,
the old trees.

Fire in Enfield

Most days
the barn stands
across the street
from the washette,
high empty
windows staring into space
of another century.

Today, the barn's
on fire. People
roused from
the sleeping tenement
stand shyly among
their valuables:
a vacuum

cleaner, somebody's golden
reclining chair,
blank TV's.
Hope it don't
burn is
in their eyes.
Everybody here watches

water
from two hoses
unravel into the fire
like string.
The flames
do not hurry.
They belong here,

what the fat
man, tattoo blossoming
on his arm,
perhaps knows.
The great
old roof
is open;

flames
take the air
like sails.
Skinny kids
watch the barn
sink slowly
into the earth.

Leaving the Country House to the Landlord, Five Years Later

Outside, the landlord undertakes the landscape
while he waits. He is ignoble
in his T-shirt, jiggles
a little above the taut power
of his mower.

But he gets things done.
When he puts his chain saw once
into our shade tree, it twists and falls.
Its branches look up startled
from the ground.

Inside, I curse him for coming.
It is in the dining room.
Blank walls undo the voice of my anger;
you look up from naming boxes
and shrug.

Behind you a hook has left
a hole open like a mouth.
I half see it, the way, taking out
boxes, I notice your writing thin as tendril
and misspelled.

His family drives in.
The car is in love with size,
wanders into the front lawn by our truck
and stops: its chrome grille tips and grins.
There's the big wife

who came at supper once when light was amber
on our table and our books lay
behind glass in another room and the cats
riffled their bright fur, telling us how
she'd fix the place.

The children watched her flat voice hang

in the air. It was as if they were dreaming
she was there, they were so awed.
Closing a door on upside-down dining chairs,
I, too, am dreaming.

And the dream goes on. It will not stop; I can't awaken.
We are still moving out of the old cape.
In the front yard another tree
has foundered. It leans on one side like
an exhausted fish.

The family outside seems underwater,
moving onto the floor of the new space.
Slowly, the boyfriend is bumping the strange, angry
saw against a branch. Blue smoke blooms
and rises.

The daughter is pleased—her sane
skin wavers in the light. The wife
is too big. In a kinder dream
she might lift slowly upward
carrying her clear

modern window planned for the upstairs
far beyond the upstairs. But here
she just remains too big
and does not budge from earth.
Meanwhile, the landlord

judges in his baseball cap the calves
of the boy, how well they know
a motor. He is at home
with enterprise and things that go,
and when he shouts

commands that drift sleepy as bubbles,
inaudible above the raging saw,
we both can hear them say:
"You are awake. And what you've dreamed
are your five gentle years."

20

Memory of Kuhre

—killed by a tractor, August 1969

hot days the farm
does not move
far off
a cowbell far off
his tractor sound
caught in trees
and free again

I am there unsurprised
by my skinny arms
raking in a field
I think maybe it will rain

but the clouds
move slowly they
are in another country
at dusk the cows move back
into the field like clouds
they dream themselves
walking shaking flies
from their sleep

mornings the woman
who talks to the hens
throwing seeds

and it is me listening
deep into the tractor's
ponderous heart
for a spark
pulling the flywheel

I think
(it starts
up in such a rage)
how can the old man
hanging crutches
on the gearshift
climbing slowly
up its side
not be shaken down

but each day
Kuhre just lurches off
into the tractor's noise

and oh it is such
a great slow place
the cows moving back
the clouds far as continents
his tractor circling
all my afternoons
and I am perhaps thinking
his eye is gone

at supper the woman crazy
with questions
I am thinking it

still Kuhre sits
silent and one-eyed
as his old barn
and he never answers
he never

riding out past cows
dreaming him riding
or it could be Kuhre's
strange shut face
going by me
while I rake

until I think part
of him knows something
it is night or down
in a dim green silo
corn raining all around
I rise slowly upward
toward the light

and the morning rises
it will be a hot day
far off
the tractor sound
continues and the clouds
just continue

and it is me
watching the woman among
the white shrieking
of the hens throwing seeds
talking to them all

Mina Bell's Cows

O where are Mina Bell's cows who gave no milk
and grazed on her dead husband's farm?
Each day she walked with them into the field,
loving their swayback dreaminess more
than the quickness of any dog or chicken.
Each night she brought them grain in the dim barn,
holding their breath in her hands.
O when the lightning struck Daisy and Bets,
her son dug such great holes in the yard
she could not bear to watch him.
And when the baby, April, growing old
and wayward, fell down the hay chute,
Mina just sat in the kitchen, crying "Ape,
Ape," as if she called all three cows,
her walleyed girls who never would come home.

Going Back to Fifth Grade

Hair on Television

On the soap opera the doctor
explains to the young woman with cancer
that each day is beautiful.

Hair lifts from their heads
like clouds, like something to eat.

It is the hair of the married couple
getting in touch with their real feelings for the first time
on the talk show,

the hair of young people on the beach
drinking Cokes and falling in love.

And the man who took the laxative and waters his garden
next day with the hose wears the hair

so dark and wavy even his grandchildren are amazed,
and the woman who never dreamed minipads
could be so convenient wears it.

For the hair is changing people's lives.
It is growing like wheat above the faces

of game show contestants opening the doors
of new convertibles, of prominent businessmen opening
their hearts to Christ, and it is growing

straight back from the foreheads of vitamin experts,
detergent and dog food experts helping ordinary
    housewives discover

how to be healthier, get clothes cleaner, and serve
dogs meals they love in the hair.

And over and over on television the housewives,
and the news teams bringing all the news faster
and faster, and the new breed of cops winning the fight
against crime, are smiling, pleased to be at their best,

proud to be among the literally millions of Americans
    everywhere
who have tried the hair, compared the hair, and will never
    go back
to life before the active, the caring, the successful,
    the incredible hair.

The Bald Spot

It nods
behind me
as I speak
at the meeting.

All night
while I sleep
it stares
into the dark.

The bald spot
is bored.
Tired of waiting
in the office,

sick of following me
into sex.
It traces
and retraces

itself,
dreaming
the shape
of worlds

beyond its world.
Far away
it hears the laughter
of my colleagues,

the swift sure
sound of my voice.
The bald spot
says nothing.

It peers
out from hair
like the face
of a doomed man

going blanker
and blanker,
walking backwards
into my life.

Don Greenwood's Picture
in an Insurance Magazine

Greenwood's picture,
taking me into my dream
of childhood where
teachers wore blue hair
and the earth
was in the principal's room. He

would not recall
their solemn
noses and windowsticks
ready against
unpleasant odors. But there
was Greenwood always

elaborately solemn
who was also good
with mothers (he could play
it serious or
chubby depending
on the occasion). Don Greenwood's

picture in an insurance magazine!
Skilled winner
of badges, old captain
of the safety patrol
in a country outside the pink continents
of my dream

of geography! In a
full-
page mosaic
of zealous frowns and sinewy grins and
repetitious ears
Greenwood

has dropped
the baby fat and got down
to solider stuff. He
is confident in his mastery
of the facts
of life and death and O

I look at his strange
face, still
thinking into the dream
he does not recall
and of
unpleasant odors

our so solid
teachers somewhere
in their world
(mapless
and windowless)
could not stop.

Going Back to Fifth Grade

You sit down
close to the floor
losing your height forever.
All along they have been
expecting you. Across the aisle a boy
with thick glasses and
wide underwater eyes
turns to smile. You become aware
that he is not happy,
that none of them are happy.
The baby-faced girl
with breasts and the bald one
off by the windows who had ringworm
are blaming you
with words you can't quite
catch. Surely they recall your painting
of the tropical bird
you ask, speaking their names
which you have never forgot.
But things get worse: Someone is questioning
your decision to grow up
in the first place, leaving them here.
The whole class applauds.
Up front, meanwhile, the Penmanship Man
who travels all over the state
writing beautifully
is putting on his coat,
and the teacher is at the blackboard
dotting the *i* in your name
so hard her flesh jolts.
You are the Person
Who Always Spoils It
For Everyone Else. If you could make

one half-inch margin, you cry, just one
beautiful pink map
of Asia. Outside it is beginning
to rain. When you stay after school
nobody is there.

The Thugs of Old Comics

At first the job is a cinch like
they said. They manage to get the bank teller
a couple of times in the head and blow the vault door
    so high
it never comes down. Moneybags line the shelves
inside like groceries. They are rich, richer
than they can believe. Above his purple suit the boss
is grinning half outside of his face.
Two goons are taking the dough in their arms
like their first women. For a minute nobody sees
the little thug with the beanie is sweating drops
the size of hotdogs and pointing
straight up. There is a blue man flying
down through the skylight and landing with his arms
crossed. They exhale their astonishment
into small balloons. "What the," they say,
"What the," watching their bullets drop
off his chest over and over. Soon he begins to talk
about the fight against evil, beating them half to death
with his fists. Soon they are picking themselves up
from the floor of the prison. Out the window Superman
is just clearing a tall building and couldn't care less
when they shout his name through the bars. "We're
    trapped!
We got no chance!" they say, tightening their teeth,

thinking, like you, how it always gets down
to the same old shit: no fun, no dough,
no power to rise out of their bodies.

Holding the Goat

holding the goat is when the man who appears
to be my father is pulling a hammer
out of the sky again
and again and the goat is on its knees
and cannot remember why the man is pulling
the hammer which it
forgets and forgets
down among its slack legs
bleating pleasantly in a dream
of a man pulling a hammer down
from the sky popping its eyes out
emptying its tongue
dumping its body
into my arms holding the goat

When Superman Died in Springfield, Vermont

they come out of the houses of the project already
forgetting the doors they have just
opened looking upward at the boy who jumps
out of the trees and do not even know they are
beginning to run the stomachs of the men riding
up and down under their t-shirts the women's
breasts jogging they are running beyond
the sad gray porches faster than the cars
up on blocks and the father has forgotten
his voice which is swearing the same word and the mother
    far
out in front is lifting her arms above her head again
and again as if she were flying

The Faces of Americans in 1853

The Faces of Americans in 1853

for Sacvan

Let us analyze the American. . . . The American head
is generally large, which the phrenologists attribute to
increased development of the brain. There are all varie-
ties of face, though the oval predominates. . . . The fa-
cial features are, for the most part, more sharply chi-
selled with us than with any other people.
—"Are We a Good-Looking People?" (1853)

When you turned
to the farmhand who hailed you
from the field you could see the face
of the American.

Everyone had the face.
There was an appreciation
for the way each chin perfected
an oval.

All day in his shop
the blacksmith
swung his hammer laughing
at the nondescript faces of Europe.

At night in her home
the mother
admired the heads
of her children, already large.

41

As far away
as Kansas
their chiselled features rose
up from the horizon.

Indians who looked down at the faces
of those they had killed
with their arrows
wept at their mistake.

The Last Peaceable Kingdom

(painted by Edward Hicks in 1849)

for Don and Jane

By recreating his beautiful animal dream he was able to forget the
elusiveness of his ideal in the world, to erase his despair. If individ-
ual men could not transcend their weaknesses and live happily to-
gether, the animals he imagined could.
—"Animals in American Art: Edward Hicks"

Mostly they recall nothing. The bear just
nudges the cow and feels foolish
to be wearing claws and the young lion
continues on his way with the child. Still
there are times the leopard remembers.
Behind his tranquil eyes he sees
himself running somewhere out of his body.
And there are times the wolf lifting his fine
brown head can hear a scream
that seems to come from his own throat. Yet
it is quiet here and in the light
beyond them Penn rises with Indians
as if he were their thought. Nearby the ox
the old lion forgets that he is doomed
to browse the luminous hay forever.

Fitz Hugh Lane Goes to the Mast-Head

The artist came to American nature as a pilgrim . . .
primarily concerned with revealing its spiritual con-
tent. . . . On one occasion Lane [whose legs were para-
lyzed] was hoisted up by some contrivance to the mast-
head of a vessel lying in Gloucester Harbor in order
that he might get some particular perspective that he
wished to have.
—Fitz Hugh Lane

Somewhere in California miners rise
up from rocks

to massacre the Pomos.
Already you are higher,

wearing the face
that never could undo

its worry:
it is you who pass

the neat roofs
of the companies, leaving

uncounted barrels of fish and all
the merchants plotting

sea-routes to the West.
You are going straight up

past the white solemn
spires of churches,

and oh it is so beautiful to
lose your legs

and to forget the Indians
who fall deeper

and deeper,
crying out for height

until the ship's sails open
behind you like wings,

and you can see
Gloucester Harbor and everything

beyond it
never happened.

The Poetic License

On the poetic license it is the nineteenth century.

A ship named *Conventional Poetry*
is just sinking on the horizon.

Nearby in a lifeboat
Form and Vision shake hands holding the strings
of balloons between their lips.

In the balloons are words of enthusiasm about sailing to
    America,

the country where dawn is breaking and the Muse
    collapses
on the grave of Washington,
naming the states.

Her balloon is so large it grazes the face of the farmer
plowing far off in the field.
He goes right on waving,

songs come out of the mouths
of his wife and children,

out of the mouths of pioneers watching the figure of
    Columbia
lift off the prairie and rise
half out of her robe.

Oh Burgeoning Art
Oh Poetry Yet To Be, they say,
pointing to her breasts

that part the clouds,
pointing to the clouds,

pointing to my name inscribed across the West in
    longhand.

Rufus Porter, Itinerant Muralist and
Inventor, Undertakes a Commission
in Bradford Center, N.H.

In 1824,
having left a volcano to erupt
in the middle of a hunting scene
in East Jaffrey,
you arrive. The citizens

are scarcely
more surprised than your hunter, continuing
on with his dog
as smoke curls
above his head.

Nobody
comes out of the doors
of the three houses. In a leaning
shed the blacksmith
keeps up a slow

ringing sound
that dies in the fields.
In short, the place
is perfect. Fabulously
static

like farm towns
you walked through in New York,
imagining your Great
Dirigible Airship lifting
off Saint Helena

with Napoleon.
Here in Bradford Center
you begin to think
about setting free
the walls:

Boats cross your mind,
there is a red house
with a yellow door. Whole rooms open
into trees. You turn
to your assistant

with eyes that are not mad
exactly. "It's the best damn thing since
East Jaffrey," you tell him.
Then you talk about
paint.

Rufus Porter by Himself

for Jean Lipman

My fathers made Boxford, Massachusetts. They drove out
   the trees
then straightened and smoothed the land
like bedsheets. They were proud to call themselves
the first settlers. Once when I was fifteen, imagining
   myself
inside a coat and vest and static beard,
I stepped out of that body and walked
to Maine. There, looking upward past the roofs
of Portland, I found that god-damned tower.
Lord, what a sight! A flag calmly unwrapping
the sea-breeze, the windows spiraling
high above the town. When I traveled its stairway,
the light leapt and leapt for me
until I could see Casco Bay and clear
to Paris. Here, I told myself, here is a place
where I can live. And so I stayed in Portland,
becoming a house and sign painter,
sleigh-painter, drum-painter, drummer,
fiddler, schoolteacher, gristmill-builder, and a member
of the Portland Light Infantry, in five years. Then
something big happened. I was on my way
down through New York State, pulling a cartload of
   paints
behind me and trying to figure how
to free Napoleon from the island of Saint Helena,
when I envisioned a blimp. There it was,
lifting off a hayfield and rising higher
than the Portland Observatory in no time flat;
then sort of pausing to turn and float
the light. Good God, it was beautiful! Fitted out
with a rudder, a steam-powered propeller and,

last but not least, a saloon which contained the small
smiling faces of Napoleon and yours truly. I shouted
for a full minute before I noticed the farmers
in the road, leaning on their scythes.
How could I tell them I had just begun to invent
the future? I kept right on going
through New Jersey, painting portraits
and considering how to put the American farmer
on wheels. For the next several years it gave me pleasure
to imagine his solemn figure seated
on a Rotary Plow, an Engine for Harrowing, Sowing and
    Rolling
at the Same Time, and a Car for Removing Houses and
    Other
Ponderous Bodies. My favorite invention, however,
was not a farm machine or my walking cane that unfolded
into a chair or even my three-wheeled steam carriage
controlled by reins: it was the blimp.
The fact is, I chased that god-damned balloon
through five decades, trying to find someone who could
    see
the sense of it. Once, in 1849, I even wrote it up
as "R. Porter & Co.'s . . . Aerial Transport for the Express
Purpose of carrying passengers . . . to the Gold Region
and back in Seven Days . . . for $50." Of course, I lied
about everything. There was no company,
there was no blimp, there was, in short,
only me, Rufus Porter, feeling so damned free
in my mind I was on my way to California
already. Thinking of me, imagine that flight

upward, beyond the immovable farms,
beyond whole towns clinging to earth, beyond the earth.
Imagine me standing up to shout among the clouds
    forever.

Where I Live

Memory of North Sutton

Five thousand miles from here
North Sutton is sleeping.
Gas pumps doze

by Vernondale's store.
Old farmhouses lie
tethered to the road.

How quiet they are.
Holding the darkness
still in their windows,

resting their great roofs
among the trees.
Slowly, slowly they shift

their white sides
in the moonlight.
In a sound sleep

the church
lifts its stopped clock
into the night sky.

—*Chile, 1978*

After the Ice

Suddenly, the town
as it was before
the season of ice:

trees, deeper
than anyone
can remember,

ancient farmhouses
resting on stone—
and in the field,

taking the first
sun, two
lost Buicks

standing shoulder
to shoulder, hay
still in their mouths.

The Man

Inside the old body
of Mr. Brown
is a man pulling
him up
onto the backhoe
closing his fists
all nail
and knucklebone
on the great wheel. He
knows why
each day
Mr. Brown rides its
yellow thunder
around his yard
removing the lawn.
He knows why
Mr. Brown is making
his driveway deeper
and deeper.
He sees in the mounds
rising higher
than the house
a kind
of dream
of the redeemed land
of North Sutton,
New Hampshire,
U. S. A.

Thinking About Carnevale's Wife

The only sign
advertises TIRE   ALE
at Carnevale's garage.
Carnevale himself
stands under his sign
when you drive in,
waiting for your window
to reach him,
watching your tires. "Hello,
Dad," is what Carnevale says,
his business way of
disguising a bad memory.
I picture Carnevale
calling each of his children
"Dad," there are so many,
the oldest off fondling
their first
used cars, the youngest nearby
playing with hubcaps.
And when the red
gas pump begins to groan
and spin its eye
and Carnevale sings
in his unusually fine
tenor voice about lost love,
I usually think about
Carnevale's wife.
I have never seen her.
The open hoods
of cars in the grass
outside her house
utter no clues
about who's inside. Sometimes I think

she listens behind her blinds
to Carnevale singing
while he pumps gas—a large woman
with a combustible
heart. Or
that it is washday
and she—a small, tired
woman—empties
all the family pockets
of bolts and piston rings.
Or I think that she is thin
and purposeful
and waits
for vats of Carnevale
TIRE   ALE
simmering on the stove.

Calling Harold

Together
at the window
our two half-grown
female kittens,
suddenly long-necked
and deep-eyed,
stare all day
calling Harold,
Harold, over
and over.

A Dream of Herman

for Diane

I was driving the old Dodge wagon
again, with Coke cans rolling
to the front at stop signs,
and you rubbing the dash
every so often to thank the car
for not needing the spare tire
we hadn't fixed. We were on a trip
that felt like going to your father's camp, only
we never got there and didn't care.
It was a beautiful day, just enough wind
coming into the back to make the kids
squint with pure pleasure
as it scribbled their hair, and your mother
patted them, saying what a nice ride it was
in the odd, small voice
she used only for your father.
It was then in the rearview mirror I saw him,
wearing the brown cardigan he always wore
and putting on the shining bell
of his saxophone as if just back
from an intermission. You were smiling,
and suddenly I saw the reason
we were traveling together
and did not want to stop
was Herman, who just sat there
in the cargo space, breathing the scale
until the whole family sat back
in their seats, and then he lifted his sax
and opened one more song as wide
and delicate as the floating trees.

Trees That Pass Us in Our Cars

They were not made
for such travel,
yet see in the wide field
how they stir,
how they shake themselves
free of the hill
and walk toward us,
opening their great branches
as they pass. See how they lead
the white town out
to the road, carrying leaves.

Country People

Driving on winter nights
you find them

behind curtainless windows
going about their business:

the old man stooping
at his television set,

the fat woman resting
in a flowered chair

by the stove.
Their houses, great ships,

drift backward marvelously
in the new snow.

Where I Live

You will come into an antique town
whose houses move apart
as if you'd interrupted
a private discussion. This is the place
you must pass through to get there.
Imagining lives tucked in
like china plates, continue driving.
Beyond the landscaped streets,
beyond the last colonial gas station
and unsolved by zoning,
is a road. It will take you
to old farmhouses and trees
with car-tire swings.
Signs will announce hairdressing
and nightcrawlers.
The timothy grass will run beside you
all the way to where I live.